DISCLAIMER / LEGAL NO*

The information presented in this eBook represents the views of ... sher as of the date of publication. The publisher reserves the rights to alter and update their opinions based on new conditions.

The Publisher has strived to be as accurate and complete as possible in the creation of this eBook, notwithstanding the fact that he does not warrant or represent at any time that the contents within are accurate due to the rapidly changing nature of the Internet.

While all attempts have been made to verify information provided in this publication, the Publisher assumes no responsibility for errors, omissions, or contrary interpretation of the subject matter herein. Any perceived slights of specific persons, peoples, or organizations are unintentional.

In practical advice books, like anything else in life, there are no guarantees of income made. Examples in these materials are not to be interpreted as a promise or guarantee of earnings. Earning potential is entirely dependent on the person using our product, ideas and techniques. Readers are cautioned to reply on their own judgment about their individual circumstances to act accordingly.

This eBook is not intended for use as a source of legal, business, accounting or financial advice. All readers are advised to seek services of competent professionals in legal, business, accounting, and finance field.

Table Of Content

Introduction	04
Chapter 01: Materialistic Happiness	07
Chapter 02: Constant Urge Of Hustle	12
Chapter 03: Lack Of Mental Strength	17
Chapter 04: Distanced Relationships	23
Chapter 05: Wrong Attitudes And Belief	28
Chapter 06: Natural Limitations	34
Chapter 07: Negative Environment	40
Step-By-Step Guide To Becoming A No-Limit Person	46
Chapter 08: Enjoy Small Pleasures In Life	47
Chapter 09: Create A Gratitude List	52
Chapter 10: Sit In A Positive Company	57
Chapter 11: Manifest Your Dreams	62
Chapter 12: Indulge In Mental And Physical Exercise	68
Chapter 13: Rebuild Your Motivation	75
Chapter 14: Acknowledge Your Internal Feelings	81
Chapter 15: Give Yourself A Due Rest	86
Conclusion	88

Introduction

Hi reader,

Have you ever felt incomplete? Do you think your life is taking wrong turns?

Depression is widespread in today's world; it leads to the growth of untainted dejection in a person's spirit. The problem isn't restricted to specific individuals alone; it has crept into all segments of society.

All of us face setbacks; these failures aren't necessarily connected to economic losses but may involve social and familial problems. The defeats convince us to give up on our goals and commit to the pre-set standards.

It is easy for our mind to believe in barriers; these are limits that the mind can't think ahead of. Usually, they are disguised as impossible. But, only when a human reaches eternally close to them do they realize the ultimate potential of a human body and the achievability of the goals.

However, the problem doesn't start with the reluctance to surpass the limits; instead, it mainly lies in the lack of acknowledgment. Mental barriers are simply limiting beliefs that prevent humans from achieving their goals and fulfilling their potential.

In a turn of events, I found myself in a Sri Lankan village, where I was staying for some time. Elephants are pretty common in the region, and it isn't a rare sight to see them walking on roads. Once, I saw a young man carrying more than five elephants with him; all he had was a rope tied to their feet.

I was shocked at how a thin rope controlled an elephant that could practically destroy a building on its own. I questioned the guy about it, and he gave me an answer that taught me how human psychology works.

"When these elephants were born, we tied the rope to them; it was enough to control them at the time. Hence, as they grow up, they feel that they can't break past it, and we never have trouble controlling them with it."

Sometimes, we overrate the strength of our limitations; we think they are unbreakable like the rope; we are deluded into believing that a human body can't surpass its challenges, but in fact, all our constraints are thin ropes that have occupied our mental capabilities.

Once we can believe in "no limits," our mind can strive to achieve impossible goals.

However, speaking about the topic is far easier than achieving it. Numerous constraints prevent us from achieving our goals. We live in a social world where our surroundings have an impact on our behavior and motivation.

A good smile from a neighbor can cheer our day, while a honk can make it worse. Similarly, the negative thoughts in our environment can also toll our mental health. They can prevent us from growing from our shells or being better at our struggles.

Nevertheless, sometimes our body needs to strengthen its belief; it is unexpected to think that you can keep on with the same motivation after constant failures- the deeper you go, the worse it becomes.

A sigh of relief and a break to revive is more necessary than the struggle and will possibly produce better results than otherwise.

Growing into a limitless person is difficult, but the reward is worth the struggle. It may be difficult to believe that you can tune into a frequency where your body shall free itself from the shackles and run past to achieve your dreams.

In this book, we will take you through a step-by-step guide to turning into a limitless person. I understand that the first step in growth is the acknowledgment of problems; thus, we will start with the most common constraints that trouble a human mind, and in the later section, we shall talk about how you can move past your mental barriers to be a better version of yourself.

Chapter One
Materialistic Happiness

From a very young age, the people we see carrying mobile phones, wearing stylish watches, and having a lot of gadgets in their possession, we deem them as rich people or people with a lot of money. We start considering them as a benchmark in life as they have hold of everything in life, and that is how everyone should be. We develop this kind of thinking in ourselves that glorification is what is admired by a vast amount of people in the world. We construct this kind of thinking because we are in the learning, grooming phase of our lives; we do not understand that much in that particular stage, and what is admired by a lot of people is what attracts us the most.

At that specific stage, we do not think very deeply, nor do we know how to evaluate one's persona; our eyes only see what possessions do they own. In short, the MATERIALS are what we really see. But as we grow, we start realizing things in a lot of masses while, some of us grow out of such thinking, others make up a mind to go after materials as they define their personality without knowing they are leading their life to a very unorthodox life.

It is nice to be a little materialistic, but heavily relying on materials like they are the only source of happiness is utterly wrong. Some people think that life is only good and acceptable when you have money, cars, or social media followers. One big problem with materialism is that one starts to believe that only physical ease and materials can bring one happiness over fulfilling spiritual values because most people along the way forget that there is a spiritual realm present. Addiction or excessive attachment is not adequate for health - it is said that addiction can kill you, and if we talk about affection, too much of it is also troublesome. Materialism is just that. Let's clear one thing out before some of you may get really confused about what we are talking about, buying stuff that you adore is not you being materialistic.

Let's suppose you earn good money now, and you have always wanted to start a business; you always wanted to become an entrepreneur, and after everything you have been through, you decide to start a business. Now, this is not you being a materialistic person, but if you are starting a business because you want to earn more money, you want to become more moneyed than others, then it is you being materialistic.

Another example to clear this whole thing out would be, let's say, the new iPhone 13 came out, and you want to buy it because you want to upgrade your phone because you need it for work, and you are a big fan of the brand, you see, buying something for yourself and basic needs is not materialistic at all, but if you are purchasing the iPhone 13 to become cooler, to show others, even though you have a nice phone, but you want other people to know that you have money, and you stay updated with the future, then you are being materialistic.

It is as simple as explained. Buying something to make others feel impressed is a definition of a person following materialism, but buying something you love for yourself is not. In the end, it is just the intention, the mindset you have set. Such people grow a mindset that only money can buy you happiness. When you are doing something for others, you start forgetting about yourself. You start forgetting what you really love because you have all the attention towards what others may like or what would make you feel.

The thing is, money cannot buy you happiness. People may have developed materialism, but they soon will see its repercussions. Materialism is a target that never leaves your back unless it sucks all the happiness out. According to the research, materialism deteriorates your relationships, healthy environment, positivity, and happiness. Materialistic people get so indulged in making others impressed that they forget to make bonds. You will mostly find materialistic people not practicing gratitude. According to the study, they are always less grateful and happy because their intention or purpose ends. It starts and ends with making more money. That is it. No one enjoys the company of materialistic people because they do not hold any particular purpose; they become less social, more self-centered, and incompetent because their only intent becomes to compete with people and win.

Slowly and gradually, they start drowning in sadness, depression, and loneliness because everything around them starts to feel fake. Materialistic people's world revolves around acquiring possessions, and this is how they determine happiness, knowing nothing about it. Happiness comes from an outcome, from after what you have achieved. Happiness comes from being around real people who love you for who you are and not for who you pretend to be. You can find what materialism means just by looking at the word; its meaning is hidden inside it.

Buying stuff does not make people happier if that were the case, materialism would have had led many people to happiness. Materialistic people forget about their psychological needs. We need good communication, connections, and bonds to be mentally sound. Satisfaction, gratitude comes from doing something for yourself, from finding yourself. Materialism gives a false hope that buying items, making others impressed is making you awesome, admirable person, but slowly, people start to lose interest in such individuals.

This happens because materialistic people see competitiveness and this makes them less social. We humans like to take part in fun, healthy, positive conversations, conversations that teach us and not demotivate us. When you make your life's purpose to go after material, you are only left with it. If we talk about hedonic adaptation – it says that people return to their baseline level of happiness after sometime. For example, you were 75% happy when you asked your parents to get you a gaming console. After getting the very thing you wanted, after using it for a month, you will adapt to it and return back to that 75% level of happiness. This is hedonic adaptation.

A life that solely revolves around materials will only face depression, melancholy, and loneliness. Materials give you limited-time joy that finishes right after you have acclimated with them. Despite making real-life friends, you invest yourself into things that you will not even make you satisfied with your life. Give a kid three gifts; he will open his first gift and immediately move on to the second and then to the third. In the same way, materials can do that to you.

Underprivileged people dream of being rich, thinking they would be happy then, but they still watch rich people being sad, depressed, and you know why? Because the answer is simple, emotions cannot be bought. There are some things in life that you can never buy, and that include good mental health, a spouse, great relationships, and a good gathering of people. These are things that you need to lead a free life. What is the point of having materials when you are the only one enjoying them at the end of the day? Always remember that excitement does not last forever, and materialism only gives you excitement, hollow happiness.

Restriction free life requires a vast number of new experiences and risks; it is about going beyond. Materialism does not help you in leading a free life in any way. Materialistic people only carry one vision, and it is to collect materials and items. They live in a bubble; they have this false illusion that it will keep them going on in life. Restriction free life requires no constraint in the first place. Free life means putting no limitation on oneself. Living in a bubble, circling your way through life, is positioning yourself in a loop. When you go over the same routine, you start to lose the fuel you have in yourself, you run out of thoughts, and you start going into depression.

A human being likes diversity; a bit of variation in the routine. When you achieve a life's goal, you move on to the next. After starting your life's long dream, a business, you move towards the phase where you start thinking about how should you launch your business or what change should you make with your business; this is how life works. Materialistic people start developing a loop where they run around circles and go after materials thinking they will have a position in the world. No doubt, buying materials is not entirely a bad thing, but to buy materials with the sole reason to impress others, to make standing, is wrong.

Loop forms boundaries, and they put out limitations for one. Limiting your life's intent and values are you being the one putting restrictions on your own life. A free life requires ambitions, bright thoughts, good relationships, and no limitations to stop you or hold you down to a rough road or a loop.

Chapter Two

Constant Urge of Hustle

The world has evolved a lot; it has been through a lot of changes. In today's world, today's trend is tomorrows to avoid. Today's fashion is obsolete tomorrow. The world has grown competitive; the lifestyle has become so diverse and fast-paced that people look to make it into the world. The lifestyle has become so competitive that people now yearn for success more than ever.

Everyone wants to become a successful person, everyone wants the life they wish for, and everyone seeks richness. You do not reach your goals with wishes only. In today's competitive world, people are adapting to the hustling culture; it is slowly becoming a standard in today's world. Hustle culture is becoming common among students because today everyone wants to earn money.

The positive thing about all of this is that today's generation acknowledges hard work; they know how to reach success and meet their destiny. However, hard work and hustling are different. Hustling means to work and work; hustling culture promotes workaholism, to work as much as you can. Many colleges and university students are adapting to this hustling culture as well. They like to find jobs, earn money, and devote their days to constant work.

Hustling culture may be on the rise, with many thinking it improves productivity and undertaking without realizing it slowly damages and restrict you from having a free life. However, hard work is a bit different than a hustling culture. Hard work does not mean any breaks or you have to work for 24 hours. Hard work does not mean constant work.

Hustling is all that - to work, to devote yourself to working with no breaks. Hustling culture says that there is no time present; you have no time available, only work, work and work if you really want to make a place in the world. Look, hustling is not bad; it is taking hard-working to an upper level.

You can work hard in hours, let's say, you are appointed at a place where your working timings are 8:00 am to 4:00 pm, in the timeframe you can work hard for as long as you want. Hustling is quite different; hard work and hustling will get you to the finishing line, and both will make you reach the level you want to achieve, but both are quite different.

Hard work says work hard in a scheduled time, and after that, have a good night's sleep. Working hard says to work towards your goal with thinking, to have a meek approach towards going after your goals. Hustling says to just go for it, to get jobs, earn money, and do as much as you can to earn and make something out of yourself in the future.

It has become a philosophy, a mindset of the generation that hustling is the key. In hustling, your mind always remains active; it grows the habit of producing ideas and ideas - it is good that you stay active, but in doing so, you miss out on many other things. You start disregarding, minimizing sleep, your diet, meetups, and other healthy relationships.

Your brain needs a break; your soul and body require time off - even a machine, in the end, needs oiling. What happens if you do not lubricate a machine? It gets rusty, and its outcome is damaged. In the same way, when a human body overworks and works way more excessive hours, it weakens.

You may have seen in your circle that the people who work two jobs or work a full-time job always seem so stressed or edgy - it may seem that way because the workload takes a toll on the mind. If we talk about the negative attributes of the hustling culture, it lacks a lot. For one, it lacks balance. In life, if you do not possess balance, you will, in no way, meet success.

Melanie Ruelas is a financial educator, and she says that constant hustling made her miss a lot in life; she lost an abundance of precious time in doing so. She breaks the stereotype of people saying that hustling will get where you want to be socially, financially, and mentally. Melanie says that she believed it too at some point in her life until she realized what she missed in her life.

According to her story, when she was in her 20s, she used to attend school, work two jobs, and was on some voluntary work committees. She believed that the more you work, the more happiness and success you will find in life. She used to dream of being an entrepreneur and providing the best atmosphere for her child - providing her child with necessities that she missed as a child.

Carrying the intent that she longs to have a successful life, she worked, took on jobs, and did additional work. She signed up for anything just to make a name for herself, so she could provide herself and her child the comfort she longed for. She developed a hustling mindset; she hustled every day, desiring that it would bring her life financial freedom.

When she came into her 30s, she saw and realized how weakened she got. She says that she skipped meals and worked overnight on even weekends which made her only revolve around work. Even at home, she could only think of work. She gave her best at work, but still, she could not give her best because of her health and routine; she eventually lost happiness. She says that countless hours of hustle made her look at the precious time she had lost, in which she could have had set her priorities straight about her passion and life.

If we talk about her story, there is plenty to learn. If we talk about her life, she lost her soul, herself, in pursuit of making a life for her child and herself. Her mental and physical health deteriorated, and she still could not find that freedom that life had to offer. She got so focused on only seeing herself, going way up above and beyond, that she forgot along the way what she really wanted to follow.

Her life is a perfect example of hustling and how it restricts you from free life. If there is balance present in your work life with your personal life, you will be calm, satisfied and happy. Balance means giving a right and equal proportion of time to each thing that matters in your life.

If you are dedicating yourself to hard work, then you should know how to balance your work life with your personal life. If you are dedicating yourself to hard work, then you should give yourself and your family some time too. What happened with Melanie was that she lost herself along the way. She was giving too much of herself in the end; she got exhausted and fatigued from giving more which made her reprioritize her needs.

Hustling culture has its consequences. It has a lot of negative attributes. Hustling culture makes you go ahead and work, and once you start settling into whatever job you are doing, you give yourself up to it. You end up juggling jobs, studies, and personal life that you get no time remaining to consider your goals, your aims, or your passion.

It is not that you do not progress; the fact is you progress, you earn, you grow, but the very thing you want to do, you do not make time for it. Another example to describe a negative attribute of hustling culture is that let's say, you want to become a web developer, a programmer, but you want to earn, and you do not have particular skills.

What you do know is social media marketing, and you get yourself a job. Now, you will give your all to the job; you will start getting better offers from better companies without acknowledging that you will have to juggle your college or university life, personal life, and work life. University assignments, homework, then a long working job, now tell us, how would you manage to give time to your web development? By skipping meals or sleep? Well, that would be the only way to do it.

This hustling mindset breaks you, breaks your mind, your soul. Psychology says reading or learning about a skill or craft that interests you stimulates your mind and keeps you calm and happy. We require attention from alike mind people; we necessitate a mind-body connection and a feeling of safety and security that comes from being with family or friends.

Hustling makes you miss out on these things. We truly forget who we are and what do we need. To feel out of place is the worst feeling you can get; it feels like you are nowhere. You lose the ability of what you are doing and what you want to do. You find it hard to concentrate on one thing. Balancing gets hard - everything starts to deteriorate when you have so much to do in life, and you are there solely focusing on hustling.

Chapter Three
Lack of Mental Strength

What is Free Life according to you? It is an independent life free from all tribulations and full of gratitude. You will always be a person entangled with problems, stress, or a person mentally occupied all the time if you have other people always having a target on you. Having a target on your back here does not mean having an agenda or something against you. Here it means the people who affect you, the people who are always there to say something to bring you to a comedown.

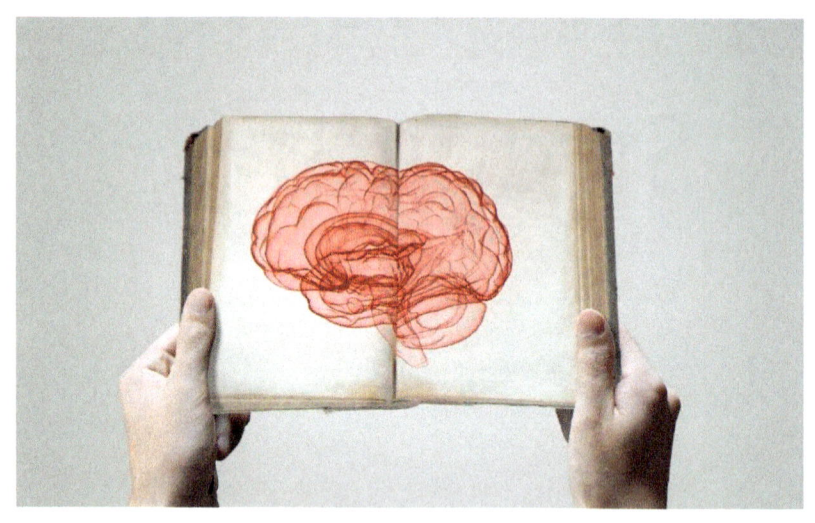

Scarcity of mental strength restricts you a lot more than you think. Not trusting yourself, being in doubt about your abilities, easily coming to terms with what others say about you - are signs of a lack of mental strength. These things leave your mind occupied because you think a little less about yourself while thinking a lot about others. It affects you by leaving you occupied and restricted within your safe area. Free life is not that you will not come across any hurdles. Free life defines independent life, having a belief, faith in oneself, a life practicing gratitude.

People with immense mentality have always seen success, and this is a fact. You lose your way and yourself in pursuit of pleasing others just because of criticism, bad remarks, or how others think of you. World-renowned actor and musician Jared Leto said sometimes you have to fight in order to be free. In the same way, people who show a robust mentality breakthrough. They do not let anybody's words drag them down; they do not care what others say.

You see, people who really pay attention to what others say and show no courage, doubt themselves, try to impress others, and hold grudges can never have a free life because they would be too preoccupied with these views. How would you be able to have a life of freedom if you already have so much weight rebelling you to go further down the road to independence?

Emotions, actions, and thoughts make up your mental strength. How you feel, how you act, and how you think are interlinked. For instance, let's suppose you are a writer who is proud of your writing and has high expectations about your work. After showing your work to some teachers, let's say, 5 out of 3 teachers criticized your work, now what would your response be after getting such comments?

A person with a strong mentality here would respect and take the criticism, and find a way to make amends and try to become a better writer instead of self-blaming, self-doubting. Now, let's go back to that example - since you had high expectations. After receiving some criticism, you felt disillusioned; you felt dejected. Since you felt that way, you started to think that you are no good, you are not cut out for writing, you lack.

Now, you will act according to the way you felt and thought, and considering your feelings and thinking, your action will be to end your passion for writing

This example was the depiction of a person lacking mental strength. Freedom knows no limitation, no restrictions; it is about not having a single thing dragging you or making you halt from achieving your goal. Freedom is about having infinite amount of positivity, productivity, and original thoughts and creativity.

Three things make up your mental strength:

Thought Process

It is all about disregarding and identifying stupid, illogical thoughts. Try to treat yourself as your well-wisher would do. Grow a habit of discouraging and substituting worse thoughts with positive and optimistic thoughts.

Emotions

Many people grow a habit of burying their feelings. The only problem that takes place is it shows that you do not acknowledge what you feel. Instead of disregarding your pain or your emotions, acknowledge them. It will help you deal with many situations because you will know about your feelings or emotions - it may even help you stay relaxed before a stressful situation.

Actions

The last is your actions. Be wary of your actions as they speak volumes; they define your personality. Mental strength revolves around positivity and productivity, which is required to sustain a free life. Your doings should be productive; this involves self-care as well.

There is a lot of perversion regarding mental toughness - many people have weird ideas about mental strength. Suppressing your emotions, not talking about your problems, or not recognizing you are hurt is not being mentally strong. Opening up about your problems, your feelings, acknowledging your feelings, opening up about your issues to someone shows strength. Even crying shows strength. A lot of people have a misconception that all of it shows weakness, but the truth is people who are mentally tough, without being hesitant, ask for help. Do not ever forget that it takes up a whole lot of mental strength to open up about problems or to cry.

If we were to put it into steps toward a free life, we would put Mental strength first because it is essential for everyone to have their mindset already made for such life. What will you reciprocate to the world, to your problems, if you do not have the sentiments for the life you want?

Mental strength is a character attribute that represents one's mindset. According to research and studies, the mental strength of an individual plays the most vital role in their development. Mentally tough people show more commitment, deliver better results, and come up with more effective solutions. They are more satisfied with their lives; they have better stress management, are more ambitious, and radiate positivity. Being open to learning new things, showing positive behavior, and having optimistic thoughts are symptoms of a person portraying strong mental strength.

Things that deteriorate your mental strength:

There are many little habits or the things we do that grow up to become a bigger problem for us. Here are some things that people do or you may find yourself doing:

Avoiding Change

You cannot ever avoid or try to shy away from change. Change is inescapable, and it is okay to fear it. But to always remain in your comfort zone and never go out of the boundary shows you do not believe in yourself.

Trying To Please Other People

What others think of you simply does not matter; you should know you do not have to prove anything to anyone. You lose your way in trying hard to please others. You diverge from your goals, from your dreams, and push yourself to find ways to make happy people. Whatever you do, it's just another way you're going to disappoint someone.

Getting Controlled By Others

It is about having control over yourself. Only you can know what you want from the inside. Sometimes, we give all the power to others; we let other people make our decisions, our choices. Individuals with a strong mentality will not give someone else the power over them. Yes, take advice and help but it's always got to be you who makes the final call. Your decisions should be yours alone.

Wasting energy on things that can't be controlled

There are certain things in life you cannot control. Incidents such as weather or heavy traffic are parts of life; you cannot control them. Ranting, complaining, and ruining your mood over such conditions is pointless. Instead of ranting about something as senseless as that, think of what you have control over and what can you do in such conditions.

Dwelling in the Past

Living in your past is a big problem that keeps you limited in everything life brings. Do not live in it but learn from it. People have the tendency to lose themselves in their glory days just because they are struggling in the current world. Focusing on the past leaves you too entangled to focus on the present, and your will to work will gradually deteriorate.

Above mentioned habits were presented to deliver you an idea about how your mental strength can be a limitation. Athletes such as Cristiano Ronaldo or Novak Djokovic are inspirational and idols to many because their mentality has secured them a place to be on the list of all-time greats. They have given top-notch performances despite being hated, booed by the crowds. If they had believed what their haters had to say about them, they would not have achieved the status they sit at now. People with strong mentality never put restrictions on their abilities, which is why they continuously thrive. If you put limitations on yourself, you have already limited your life.

Chapter Four
Distanced Relationships

From the day we are welcomed into this world, we form relations; this is how humanity works. One cannot thrive alone. One needs others to help oneself to grow and learn. All these relations you build with people help you shape your mindset, personality, etc.

We human beings are not complete until we have someone; we are not whole. Sometimes, we need others to fullfil the need we lack. Your parents, siblings all groom you just because you see them every day, and as human beings, we unknowingly adopt many things.

As you grow, mature by age, you start forming more relationships; they are either toxic or beneficial for your advancement. Relationships you build with your mom, dad, friends, teacher, or someone you love help you emotionally and mentally. To know you have someone at the end of the day calms your mind. Along the way, at some point, we do get a faraway lot of people. Sometimes, it is life that keeps us busy or some experiences that stop us from being available all the time.

Distanced relationships are sad whether you are distant from your father, mother, siblings, or spouse. Think of relationships as investments - you invest in a company and then leave it how it was running without really looking after it. At some point, the company faces its extinction, thus leaving you with regrets about how you did not do anything to keep it alive and the money you lost.

Being distant is just like that. You invest in a relationship and take what is beneficial for you. Distance in a relationship is like a border disjoining two countries, you do not get to know what is going on between the two of you, and you suffer mentally. Distance is good in a relationship.

Everyone should have their me-time, but when losing respect, lack of communication and attention takes place, that is where everything begins to go into a downward spiral. Distance holds the ability to destroy many things in your life. It can put everything you have in jeopardy.

Whenever you get distant, whether it is being distant away from studies, sports, relationships, you get rusty, you start to feel like you are losing your passion, your glimmer. Relationships require time, just like sports and studies; they are essential for survival.

There are two kinds of distances that occur in relationships; figuratively and literally. If we talk about the distance that emerges in your relationships when you move out to where you know nobody, it destroys you a bit, but it also determines how strong your relationships are with others, and it necessarily does not really restrain you from a life of freedom.

Whatever disturbs your mind or throws you off your daily regime impacts and finds a way to become resistant to achieving your goal. Toxic and distanced relationships are not further apart when it comes to restraining you from a life of freedom because both hold you down. Communication is the key; it is how we form connections.

Every relationship requires a different kind of approach to it. Let's talk about marriage - two people who love each other ties hand and vow that they will be together for the rest of their lives. They share everything and form an unbreakable bond, and in doing so, they sometimes tend to forget what balance is.

Being so busy in married life causes distance from parents or siblings; it happens because you get so busy, but when you notice or when you are reminded by your friends, siblings, or parents of how you used to be towards them, it does leave you occupied in thoughts. It affects your ability to concentrate.

Especially when you start to realize how many people you were constantly in contact with have lost touch with you because you were either too caught up to make time for them or you were the one igniting the relationship. In other words, distance occurs. The benefit comes in a way that it shows you how many dead flowers you were watering but troubles you a lot when you realize how many strong bonds you have lost.

Distrust, distance occurs in a relationship even though you are not doing anything besides unbalancing or upsetting close relations with your father, mother, friends, or siblings. You fall into deep thinking, depression, or sometimes guilt - this makes one too caught up with his own thoughts, leaving one unfocused about one's job or life. What hurts the most is when you realize the people you knew all about at one point start to feel like strangers because you get so distant.

Failed marriages are also the product of the same problem that is being distant. If we talk about the relationship that marriage is, then it is the strongest yet fragile of all the relationships because if it has to end, it ends in just a matter of months or years, but if it lasts, it lasts a lifetime.

The marriage is based on trust, a level of comfortability, same interests, and as time goes on, it develops even more. Yes, the distance can even occur in such a relation as well. The marriage starts failing gradually - the failing or decline can originate from an incident such as a demise of a parent or losing a job. Such events make one preoccupied to deal with other meaningful things.

Marriage requires communication, invulnerability, and such events can be the beginning of decline if the couple does not take any positive measures. Sometimes, the couple grows different interests or hobbies - if one starts investing one's time in a job to earn more for the family, the other one indulges in other activities, leaving no one to concentrate on home.

The same couple begins to have a dispute over small matters because no one is present to talk about the problems and how to meet up with their solutions. This lack of communication, this space, starts it all off. Distance is like a ticking bomb. What good is a relationship if there is no dispute, right?

Every couple goes over problems, but steps are taken to find the solutions; love is about compromise. Along with these circumstances come things like distrust, lack of chemistry, and all that paving the route for distance; that is when things get worse and worse until the whole relationship falls completely apart. The relationship becomes toxic and affects mental health more than everything. Distance in a relationship only stops when the two persons completely go on to their separate roads.

A failed marriage and other damaged relations throw you into a dark pit of the abyss full of negative perpetual thoughts; you start to lose all the creativity and longing to work. You lose a whole bowl of positivity, energy, and hope when you go through such relationships.

You start to lose interest in your future; you begin to refrain from working on the very thing you wanted to achieve because you are going through physical and mental exhaustion, unknowingly restricting yourself from looking at things from a broader perspective.

You feel all of this because you form attachments; you grow their habits, you evolve their existence on you, along the way, you lose yourself, you give up on everything. In life, we carry such events as luggage; they may slow us down, restrict and chain us.

Everything in life requires time, which is why the time has an impeccable reputation. A free life does not mean a life of freedom where you are doing what you want to do even if hurting others comes in the way. Free life means to live a life where you can take out all the positivity or mould all the negativity into positivity - to take all of the hatred out of yourself.

Freedom does not come from a hateful mindset instead; it comes from a loving nature. We make relations, connections so that we can feel good and not restrict ourselves from making bonds, relationships, and from opening up. Relationships are a positive change in life, such change can become toxic and injurious if not supervised. Distanced relationships may not entirely restrict us, but they keep on disturbing and deteriorating our health.

As long as you do not do anything to get closure, you will never be able to feel good; there will always be a thing dragging and restricting you down. You will never be able to reach the level you want to sit at - you can never, especially when you have an anchor producing friction, making it extra challenging for you to concentrate on yourself.

Your attitude and beliefs play a prominent role when facing all of this because your perspective towards distanced relationships can influence you in many weird ways; the approach you carry to all of this determines if you really want to be at the level, you see yourself. Many things restrict us and keep on constraining us, our beliefs and attitude can help shape all the negativity.

Chapter Five
Wrong Attitudes & Beliefs

Attitude is how you see things; it is how you view the world. Your attitude and beliefs make the world for you. Your eyes see what your mind comprehends. You can think of attitude as an evaluation you make about people, problems, or the world. Your past experiences, background, brought up, and relationships mold your beliefs and how you perceive things. It helps you develop a sense of what is right and wrong. Not everyone has same attitude or beliefs such as you; everyone has their own viewpoint, belief, attitude towards other people. You should know other people do have different attitude, values, and beliefs; you only need to learn how to cooperate with them.

One dirty and sick fish can contaminate and damage the whole pond. It is a recognized quote. It means that one can influence an entire society. Having wrong beliefs and attitudes regarding things in life may stop you from achieving what you want. We all have heard and are constantly reminded that we can accomplish anything if we put our mind to it - we often forget that our attitude demarcates the outcome and our beliefs are the ones backing it. If you think that something cannot happen, you should also know there is also a chance that something can happen. Whether you are starting a business or doing something for yourself, you should always want to have an optimistic approach to it because limiting beliefs and wrong attitudes will always be the ones keeping you in the bay.

Wrong Beliefs

We make our decisions by what we know to be accurate, in simple words, what we believe. How do we learn? We learn from our past experiences, relationships, upbringing - the things we realize from all of that impact and develop our beliefs. If you think you cannot do something, you already have put yourself under a limitation. Wrong beliefs can make you a person too fed up with negative thoughts. Let's suppose you are to host a class presentation.

If you think your classmates are going to laugh, you will not be able to host the presentation correctly. In doing so, you are missing out on an opportunity to learn, showcase your abilities - putting a limit on your potential without even seeing it. Fueling your negative thoughts only turn these thoughts into beliefs. These beliefs grow and grow to a point where you have limited yourself and your abilities. Now, even if you try doing something new, you're most likely to fail at it. That is because you have already set yourself up for failure. You will stay where you are, stopping yourself from experiencing new opportunities, and new challenges.

Some Wrong Beliefs that are holding you back:

- "I am too old"
- "I am not strong enough"
- "People will judge me"
- "I can never do this"
- "I'm not cut out for this"
- "This happened to me last time and it will happen again"

There is no denying that a wrong set of beliefs are vastly misleading and restricting. Some of our beliefs are molded by:

- Society

Society is stereotypical. It will want you to check all the boxes and if you give in to the idea that you need to fit a mold to be accepted, you have let go of your actual beliefs and you form newer beliefs that are harmful.

- Fears

We all have fears whether it's facing rejection or not being able to live up to someone's expectations. These fears instill beliefs in you that you are not good enough or never will be. Another wrong belief that is setting you up for failure.

- Personal Experiences

Traumatic experiences affect your life and the way you perceive things. Hurtful experiences form beliefs in you that are not wholly true. Life isn't fair and it's not always rewarding. Just because it went wrong once doesn't mean it will go wrong again. You deserve to heal.

- Hereditary beliefs

Some beliefs are passed on to you by your family. The people around you have their own beliefs and seeing them believe something can influence the way you think.

- Social Circle

You need to surround yourself with people who make you feel better about yourself, who inspire you to try out different things. Surrounding yourself with good people will motivate you and help you break the barrier of negative thinking.

- Judgments

You are going to be judged for everything you do and even for things you didn't do. It's time you do not let people's judgments get to you. Leave what people think to the people and do whatever you want to do. This will only hold you back and fuel wrong beliefs in you.

- Wrong Attitude

We talked about how wrong beliefs can cause an impact in our lives and how they are formed in the first place. One thing that deserves to be talked in detail is your attitude. Attitude is the way you look at things or a point of view. Remember, you are responsible of how you look at things. Once you have a wrong set of beliefs, you're bound to have a bad attitude towards a lot of things.

If you ever are seeing yourself turning down opportunities because you believe you are not cut out for them, not giving yourself a chance to try something, or not starting something new because you think it can fail. If the answer to this is 'yes' then it means you have a bad attitude. What goes around comes back around. If you have a bad attitude towards life, you are attracting wrong attitudes back to yourself.

Imagine starting a business. You believe you don't have what it takes to start one. You give it a try with the mentality that it's likely to fail (bad attitude). You are unmotivated and the business ends up flopping. Where did it go wrong?

1. Self-doubt: You have a wrong belief that you don't have what it takes to start a business. If there's a 50% chance you will fail then isn't there a 50% that you will succeed?

2. Bad Attitude: "He who thinks will lose, has already lost". With such a pessimistic approach to life, you are just helping yourself fail. It is as simple as that. Once you believe that you are going to fail, the steps you're going to make next are going to be in the favor of that. Keep a positive attitude and approach with the mentality that you will succeed and every step that you take next will be in the favor of success.

3. Bad Attitude: "He who thinks will lose, has already lost". With such a pessimistic approach to life, you are just helping yourself fail. It is as simple as that. Once you believe that you are going to fail, the steps you're going to make next are going to be in the favor of that. Keep a positive attitude and approach with the mentality that you will succeed and every step that you take next will be in the favor of success.

A loop leads you back to where you started off. Wrong beliefs steer you far from reality and cause you to form a bad attitude. This type of attitude makes you diminish all the possibilities of something ever happening. In the end, you find yourself uninterested, and you do not get it done. Now your brain jumps back to how you knew it all along that it would not work out; all of this makes your wrong beliefs grow stronger. Leaving you back where you were, just like a loop.

Attitude singlehandedly has destroyed people. Look, nobody is ever born with a bad attitude; it is something you grow along with your life through your experiences, traumas, etc. Unrealistic expectations, for one, are a big part of the problem; not meeting such expectations can lead you to a disturbed, unsettling mood. A bad attitude will always keep you in the back of beyond from obtaining a valid, unbiased perspective of life. You must have noticed people with bad attitudes usually end up being depressed, lonely or sometimes become the reason for their own limitations in life. You can take Charlie Sheen or Megan Fox as an example here.

Both actors' attitudes lost them their respect and ruined their personalities. Megan Fox was an emerging star of the Transformer Movie series, but her sloppy and non-serious attitude had her fired from the role. If we talk about Charlie Sheen, he was emerging as a mega movie star in the 80s, but his constant attitude problems, anger management issues, and then he was involved in assault and battery charges and other sexual and substance abuses. A world-renowned actor became a demise of his own just because of his wrong attitude.

If you want to ever be successful, you need to have a positive, realistic, and optimistic approach. This means you should believe in yourself and take action & steps to reach your set goals, and no matter what the result is, keep on going with a healthy attitude that you are bound to succeed. Abandon wrong beliefs like self-deprecation, self-doubt, negative framing, et cetera. Pessimistic People are known to be unhealthier, lazier, and unsuccessful.

Successful people do not host wrong beliefs, and neither do they have a negative attitude. Psychology says that people with optimistic beliefs and attitudes are mentally and physically healthier. With the wrong attitude and beliefs, instead of allowing yourself to see the freedom you want to see, you chain yourself with the wall.

Chapter Six
Natural Limitations

Multiple elements hold us back and prohibit us from living our best lives. We tend to overlook these issues, but this is primarily due to our lack of awareness of all the natural limitations that exist around us and could potentially be a roadblock in life. Recognizing these tendencies, on the other hand, is critical to being your best self and having no regrets later in life as you reflect on your accomplishments and the person you have become. Everyone constantly pushing us to live our best lives, but no one has actually given us a blueprint for how to do so. After all, since the definition of a good life is very subjective, it is entirely up to us to select how we live our lives and make them the best we can.

Self-discovery is a wonderful adventure that rewards you in a variety of ways. When you're clear on who you are, you can focus on getting what you want and becoming the absolute best of yourself. Without realizing it, we can be our own worst adversaries when it comes to living a life of purpose and passion, pursuing our aspirations, and attaining success. It is high time for us to understand and eliminate the damaging tendencies that may be causing serious limitations in our lives. It will not happen overnight, but it will be a process you will be glad you went through. The following are some of the limitations that could stand in your way of becoming the finest version of yourself.

Fear of Failure

Fear is an inevitable aspect of existence, but it does not indicate the end of the world. You are not ready to succeed if you are frightened to fail. Failure is a stepping stone to achievement, not an impediment. If you do not give up, the more times you fail, the more likely you are to succeed. Failure is a teacher; it teaches you what did not work and, if you let it, it will push you to find new ways to succeed. People who are unsuccessful allow failure to cripple them. In the face of failure, they give up and stagnate. If you want to succeed, you must overcome your fear of failing. So, analyze all possible outcomes, sketch a worst-case scenario to prepare for it, and soothe your worry.

Lack of Purpose

If you want to be successful, you must have a strategy in place. If you do not plan to succeed, you are planning to fail. When you wake up every day, you need to know why you are getting up. You must have a goal and a strategy for your life. Successful people have a strategy for their lives, a budget, and hopes and goals. You must have a good plan and a sense of direction in order to succeed in life. According to studies, people who have a distinct sense of purpose in life live longer than those who live a life without one, which goes to show how a lack of purpose can be highly unfulfilling.

Procrastination

Procrastination and success are incompatible. There is no success where there is procrastination. Procrastination is one of the biggest impediments to waking up, making the correct decisions, and living the life you've always imagined. According to recent studies, people regret the things they haven't done more than the things they have. Furthermore, regret and guilt associated with squandered chances tend to linger for far longer. All of our opportunities appear to be at our fingertips at times, yet we can't seem to grasp them. When you procrastinate, you are wasting time that could be spent on something more important. You will be able to do more and better harness the potential that life has to offer if you can defeat this formidable foe. To avoid procrastinating, make your actions calculating and exact, create some type of accountability, and set small, reasonable, and realistically attainable goals.

Low Self-Esteem

People who have low self-esteem are constantly worried about making mistakes or disappointing others. Self-esteem difficulties can have a severe impact on your health as well as your personal and professional connections. T Your own mental condition is a big contributor to low self-esteem. Even if there is proof to the contrary, your inner voice, or thoughts in your head, can be continuously telling you that you are not good enough or worth anything. Negative thinking is linked to low self-worth and self-esteem in general. Self- talk is something we all do, but it becomes self-destructive when it is loaded with unreasonable and negative thoughts. Most of the time, they aren't facts, but rather our own negative self-perceptions. So, suppress your inner critic and try to see the bright side of things. The important thing is to believe in yourself—that is all that is required. Allow no one to put you down or tell you that your aspirations are unattainable. All you need is the belief that you can succeed.

Wanting to Please Everyone

People-pleasing entails prioritizing the needs of others over your own. People-pleasers are sensitive to others' needs and are frequently regarded as agreeable, helpful, and kindhearted. On the other hand, they may find it difficult to advocate for themselves, which can lead to a destructive pattern of self-sacrifice or self-neglect. These people are prone to stress, and despair, and, most significantly, are frequently exploited. So quit being a sissy and start speaking up. Accept that you come first, that you can't make anyone happy unless you're happy yourself, and that you can't please everyone. This will help you regain your sense of self and confidence.

Finding Faults

It is fine to see a flaw, but if you want to succeed, do not stop there. Instead of whining about what's wrong with something, figure out how to fix it. Problem solvers are successful people. They spend more time trying to come up with a solution rather than grumbling about the problem.

Fear of Success

This may sound weird because why would someone be afraid to succeed? It is, nonetheless, more prevalent than we realize. Fear of success lurks in the subconscious and manifests in a variety of ways. Do you become scared when everything appears to be going well and you begin to anticipate something going wrong? People fear success because it might bring with it more expectations, increased responsibilities, and the fear of not being able to handle it. So, the next time things appear to be going well for you, keep in mind that success is a wonderful thing, and everyone deserves to live their dreams and have a great impact on the world. And deal with success by remaining loyal to yourself and being at ease with every decision you make.

Lack of Courage

Courage is the ability to act regardless of the circumstances. To be successful, you must have the guts to pursue your dream despite hurdles. Courage is the ability to make courageous decisions in the face of adversity. It is taking action in the face of adversity while expecting positive outcomes. There will always be reasons why something cannot be done, but courageous people see possibilities and find solutions. They don't let fear and intimidation control their actions and decisions. They are focused on achieving their objectives. Lack of courage can hugely impact your will to achieve your dreams so make sure you overcome it and never let it get in your way.

Ignorance

The world is always changing, and if you refuse to learn new things, you will become obsolete. Knowledge is a powerful tool. School isn't the only place where you can learn. Whatever industry you work in, you must always learn and refresh your knowledge. Learning is a habit that successful individuals have. Ask yourself if your failures aren't self-inflicted as a result of your lack of knowledge.

Failure and defeat will be your constant companions if you approach your dreams in ignorance. Make time to learn first.

Fear of Being Ridiculed

Perhaps you have specific interests that are mocked by some of your peers. In many circumstances, we are afraid that what we do, say, or like will be ridiculed and mocked by others. When it comes to the opinions of our friends and family, this dread will be amplified. You start to question your own personal attributes as you begin to wonder whether there is something odd about you. However, You have to be willing to seem stupid for a while if you want to achieve big things in life. You must accept the fact that you are not yet at the level you desire. Only by accepting yourself can you develop the constancy and honesty necessary to grow and progress.

Fear of Rejection

Unfortunately, many people lose their objectives and ambitions due to their fear of rejection. They will not pursue their talents since they do not want to be noticed. They don't take advantage of every opportunity that presents itself to them. They are terrified of losing the support of their friends and family if they start a business. To avoid being rejected, they embrace the same undesirable habits as their peers. Overall, the desire to escape the agony of rejection might lead us to act in ways that are inconsistent with our goal and purpose. It's not something to be ashamed of; it's just human nature. Only by recognizing and accepting your worries can you begin to overcome them.

Chapter Seven
Negative Environment

Our health and well-being are influenced by the physical and social environments in which we live and work. Every day, we are surrounded by a variety of individuals, and we frequently underestimate the impact they have on us, as well as how the environment we are in may either propel us ahead or hold us back. The individuals that live in a certain place shape it. People who live in a negative atmosphere are more likely to be surrounded by pessimists. It is high time for us to recognize the harmful patterns that are present all around us and contribute to a bad atmosphere.

Negative Work Environment

The basic question arising here is, what exactly is a negative environment and how do you know if you are in one? A toxic work environment is one in which the employees, the job, or the company's culture and ideals have created a toxic atmosphere. Even in the most employee-oriented firms, a bad environment may propagate, making it extremely difficult to deal with.

Employers, on the other hand, can limit the spread of negativity in the workplace by recognizing the source of the negativity and implementing the appropriate methods. The following are some of the variables that lead to a negative environment:

A Communication Gap

Even in today's global economy, when working remotely is the new normal, communication gaps can arise due to physical, cultural, geographical, and interpersonal disparities. A lack of communication, or even too much communication, might, nevertheless, damage a company's success. So how exactly does a communication gap affect your environment?

Employees will have no feeling of direction if objectives are not conveyed effectively. Employees may become detached and disengaged as a result of this. It might generate unnecessary schedule overruns when various employees in the chain receive conflicting messages. Keeping in touch with your team after hours or on weekends might lead to greater work stress and burnout.

Work Load

Employees may feel as if they are dealing with a hostile work environment that prioritizes work over their well-being if they are required to be on the clock at all times. Employees require re-energizing time in order to be more productive. Overworking has a negative impact on their emotional health, but it can also have a negative impact on their physical health. When employees have to face a work-life imbalance, they exhibit various symptoms that may disrupt their work efficiency.

For example, they might feel exhausted and stressed all of the time. Due to their increased anxiety, they may experience sleeplessness. Employees become upset as a result of such negative features of overworking, which leads to workplace toxicity over time.

Bad Leadership

Employee morale might suffer as a result of poor leadership. Employee retention suffers as a result of weak leadership, and surviving employees become demotivated, resulting in lower productivity than would otherwise be the case. A team's respect and trust may be lost if the leader is ineffective. As a result, team members would be less inclined to work for them. How do you recognize bad leadership? Bad leaders can be anything from bullies who torment other employees by picking on their mistakes. Narcissists who do not care about their coworkers or absentee leaders that refuse to take responsibility, guide their team, and expect their members to accomplish everything on their own.

Negative Employee Behavior

Negative employee behavior is another sign of a hostile workplace. Employees that are toxic do not take their jobs seriously. They frequently disrupt work and create an uncomfortable atmosphere. Furthermore, their terrible behavior de-energizes and negatively impacts the performance of other employees, as well as causing unnecessary delays. It's critical to address reckless and unprofessional behavior in the workplace right away. Otherwise, employee disintegration, cynicism, and mistrust would rise, creating a terrible workplace for everyone.

Turnover Rate

When the work environment offers nothing but dysfunction, and low morale, colleagues will begin to flee in search of a better opportunity. If your firm or department has a high turnover rate, consider it an indication of a toxic workplace.

Disrespectful Behavior

When someone acts disrespectful, it is common for others to reply in the same disrespectful way—tit for tat. As a result, disrespect develops into a poison that quickly spreads throughout a team.

Gossips

The propagation of rumors and gossip reveals a leadership team that is unconcerned about their employees' well-being and privacy. These are immature and inappropriate acts.

Lack of Empathy from the Leader

Leaders who lack empathy or compassion are often narcissists, making it difficult for them to prioritize their staff. These kinds of leaders will frequently demand that their employees prioritize work, limiting their capacity to attain work-life balance and possibly leading to burnout. Any boss who makes his or her staff choose between their profession and their wellbeing is damaging the workplace.

Fortunately, there are numerous strategies to cope with this unfavorable situation. You may try to change the bad environment into a more positive one, or you could try to get away from the toxic environment for your own good.

Look for Positive Colleagues

The individuals you hang out with at work have a big influence on your emotions and how you view your employment. Look for teammates that are upbeat, focused on their task, and willing to help when problems arise. These could be nice professionals or people that just make you chuckle.

Spending hours with these peers can help you notice the positive aspects of your workplace that you might otherwise miss. You can also create a support network by forming connections with coworkers who share your values.

Be solution-oriented

When dealing with a problem, being solution-oriented can raise productivity, boost morale, and encourage team members to be honest. Rather than attempting to establish who is to blame, concentrate on the steps you can do to remedy the problem. Focusing on solutions can help your teammates see things more positively, motivate them to collaborate, and provide them with the tools they need to succeed.

Appreciate Your Coworkers

Always treat your colleagues the way you want to be treated. Taking the time to express your gratitude to your employees might be useful. Recognize and reward team members that go above and beyond. If one of your coworkers signs a new customer, for example, congratulate them by informing the rest of your team. When teammates complete a project effectively, congratulate them, and thank them when they offer you assistance. Simply letting individuals know that you appreciate their efforts can make them feel like vital team members.

Look For Potential Opportunities

Focusing on prospective chances is one strategy to overcome difficult employment situations. If a coworker comes to you with a problem, try to turn the topic around by asking what they've done so far to tackle the situation. You can also encourage them to consider new possibilities by asking questions with a positive outcome in mind.

Be Expressive

No one is going to know what you feel unless you put it out there. If you notice that one of your coworkers is contributing to a toxic workplace, sharing your insight in a kind and non-judgmental manner can motivate them to make good changes. Remember that your coworker may not realize the impact of their actions on the workplace. Inform them of how their actions may be perceived by others and inquire if this is the message they are trying to send.

Quit if Nothing Works

Plan how to get out of this situation if your efforts do not end well. Although it may be tempting to quit your job right once if you despise it, make sure that doing so would not place you in a worse situation. Plan ahead of time and don't quit until you've found a new career or amassed enough cash to support yourself. Start talking, but first talk to your employer. Start working on your escape strategy if it doesn't work.

Negative People

Negative people are another aspect that contributes to a negative environment. It makes no difference whether we're talking about a business atmosphere or just a regular social situation with your friends and family.

Dealing with negative people—those who bring you down with their pessimism, worry, and overall distrust—can be incredibly challenging.

Constant exposure to such negativity can eat away at your positivity bank, causing you to either become negative yourself—diffident, apprehensive, and distrustful—or become indifferent, uncaring, or even cruel to the negative person.

Walking away from them is one simple solution. But, unlike the bartender with a terrible attitude or the airline agent with an anger management problem, we can't walk away from a negative parent, sibling, spouse, coworker, or friend.

Understanding the grounds behind their negativity is a more realistic strategy for coping with them. In a nutshell, practically all negativity stems from one of three deep-seated fears: fear of being disrespected by others, fear of not being loved by others, and dread of bad things happening.

A Step-By-Step Guide to Becoming a No-Limit Person

Everyone wishes to live a life free of restrictions. Many reasons often hold us back from attaining our objectives, and we are unaware of them. These variables not only obstruct our capacity to meet our needs, but they also obstruct our daily life and may permanently harm our habits if nothing is done to remove them.

People, on the other hand, are oblivious of what is holding them back and instead complain rather than attempt to identify and correct undesirable practices in their lives. Recognize the limits that are holding you back as the first step toward overcoming them. Acknowledge that you have flaws and that they are completely fixable. A little commitment surely goes a long way.

Examine yourself and identify the factors that you believe are holding you back. These include, among other things, pursuing consumerism, burning oneself out trying to achieve anything, having weak relationships, being in a negative company, and having weak mental strength. You have the capacity to control your emotions.

While it may be easier to blame others for what happens in your life, take responsibility for what happened instead. Some of the factors to eliminate these constraints are discussed here. Following them regularly will not only help you become a no-limit person but also make you feel better about yourself in general because you will realize how self-reliant and independent you can become by incorporating little habits in your life and not letting anything get in your way.

Chapter Eight
Enjoy Small Pleasures in Life

We have established happiness ideals as a result of living in the society we do. We're surrounded by a lot of preconceived notions about what types of goods will make us happy. We are made to believe that important events, such as traveling on an international trip, earning as many zeroes as possible, and obtaining that mansion with a good view, will bring us satisfaction.

To put it another way, the more money you have and spend, the happier you will be. Another widely held belief is that fame makes people happy. People believe that an actress, a musician, or a politician is more likely to be content than the average individual. Simple instances of these paradoxes include the following:

1. A person going to Italy for a vacation would be happier than a person visiting a museum in their own country.
2. Eating dinner at a five-star restaurant makes you happier than having a nice candlelight dinner at home.
3. Celebrities like Brad Pitt would be more content than local businessmen.

These approaches aren't altogether incorrect, but they unknowingly reveal a cruel and counterproductive bias against the inexpensive, readily obtainable, conventional, ordinary, and modest ways of life. The counterintuitive and upbeat feature of pleasure, on the other hand, is how strange and indiscriminate it can be.

It has the ability to decline to accompany us on the most expensive vacations. It is extremely susceptible to emotional distress, sulks, and sporadic bad moods. A quarrel over something as minor as what to eat for dinner can devastate a five-star resort's whole value proposition. Happiness, on the other hand, can be found in the most trivial of things. Breakfast on the patio, being soaked in the rain, talking to your loved ones every day, baking a cake, watering the plants, and playing fetch with your dog can all make you happy.

Appreciating what you have isn't a lax approach. However, there is no use in chasing the future unless we improve our ability to appreciate the small moments and things that are currently available to us. More fundamentally, the smallness of little pleasures isn't an analysis of how little or big they have to offer us: it's a reflection of how many excellent things the world wrongly overlooks.

A great way to look at the small pleasures and believe that these trivial moments of happiness are in fact a big joy in the making. Striving for better relationships, jobs, and personal life has taken over our existence. We believe that being unsettled and always in a state of hustle is a sign of success. However, we neglect more modest joys closer to home because we are so preoccupied with impossible standards of greatness.

This whole concept can be easily articulated by Vanderkam, a book writer, who mentioned in an interview podcast, "the thing about happiness is that small, repeated pleasures are the bread and butter of human happiness. Things like dinners out with friends, parties, enjoying a nice cup of coffee – all of these things are key components of happiness, and they make us happy over and over again, so cutting them out is very painful because it requires self- discipline every single day." Simple joys and wonderful moments are accessible to us every day if we practice seeking them out and being present in them.

After all, is said and done, how do you actually acquire the subject in question? Trying to enjoy the little things when there are bigger, better things bugging you in the back of your mind can be difficult. How can you enjoy the minor pleasures when the voice in your head tells you that you should be doing something more productive?

Every time you enjoy small pleasures, your persistent need to hustle and achieve big goals gets in the way. When this moment comes, the most important thing to do is thoroughly immerse yourself in whatever you are doing. According to research conducted, people's overall well-being improves when they can fully immerse themselves in the activity, and they suffer less anxiety and despair.

People whose minds constantly return to the goals they aren't working on, on the other hand, are unable to truly appreciate their delightful pastime. This study is very much in line with the concept of flow. Flow refers to being so absorbed in an activity that nothing else seems to matter, and the experience is so pleasurable that individuals will do it for the sake of doing it, regardless of what it takes in the process.

There are numerous ways to appreciate the small joys in life. These are moments that don't need to be created from the ground up. They are already there in our daily lives from time to time, but we are oblivious most of the time due to larger distractions. The idea is to begin noticing these small moments and boost our chances of happiness, which is feasible if we are committed enough. Below are some ideas of the everyday things you can enjoy and get the most out of.

Watching The Sunset And The Sunrise

What could be more inspiring than waking up early and staring across a natural scene as the sun rises above the horizon? After such a lovely start, you'll be sure to feel optimistic and motivated for the rest of the day. Even if your day didn't go as planned, you can always sit down to stare at the sunset later in the day and give yourself some time to forget about everything for a while.

Hugging your Loved Ones

Hugs could never go wrong. Whether you are feeling the blues because of something unfortunate or are over the moon for one of your achievements, you could always hug your best friend and cherish the fact that you have someone to share your ups and downs with.

Taking a Walk

Being outside in the fresh air is immensely helpful to our physical and mental health. Going for a walk can help us recharge, transcend our daily stresses, and rejuvenate completely. Out in nature, you'll also witness some stunning flora and animals. This will undoubtedly make you happy because it will be a welcome change from your usual commute and gridlock.

Cooking Yourself a Comfort Meal

Nothing could possibly go wrong with this. You may always go for a little breakfast before you start your day and feel good because, despite its simplicity, it is one productive approach to getting ready for the day. You may even come home from a long day and prepare some good old noodles and watch a movie to forget about your worries.

Meditation

Some people regard meditation as a chore, although it is far from that. It's an excellent technique to relieve tension and induce the release of therapeutic chemicals in your body.

Celebrating Little Things

Make it a practice to congratulate yourself on even the smallest accomplishments throughout the day. This might be as simple as completing a task or receiving praise from your supervisor. Appreciate yourself for it since it is a valid reason to be pleased with yourself.

Taking Trips with Your Friends

A road trip can help you rejuvenate more than anything else. We can almost promise that singing along to your favorite music with close pals will perk you up, no matter where you are going. Feel the breeze in your hair when you open the windows and let go.

Other simple pleasures include watering your plants, taking a hot shower after a long day, making someone smile, watching your favorite movie, treating yourself to your favorite food, spending quality time with your pets, and so forth. It takes time to establish the habit of finding happiness in the small things, but it is well worth the effort once you have. It not only makes happiness more likely in your life, but it also makes you a more upbeat person with a positive attitude on life in general.

Chapter Nine
Create a Gratitude List

While regular journaling has been shown to boost your well-being, making a point of writing down all the things for which you are grateful can elevate the experience to new heights. When you write a list of what you're grateful for everyday, you're inviting more of it into your life. Despite your differences, you grow more conscious of the good in people.

Keeping a gratitude diary is straightforward, and it just entails compiling a list of the things for which you are grateful on a given day. You can choose how long each day's list should be and how much detail you wish to include. The best part is that it's a simple habit to develop, and after a while, you'll have a library of motivating content to refer to when you need a boost.

Following are a couple of reasons why you should adopt the habit of creating gratitude lists on a daily or weekly basis in accordance with your convenience.

Instilling Positivity

When you take the time to think about the positive aspects of your life, you will automatically become more optimistic. Writing down things you are grateful for might make you feel more upbeat since you are choosing to focus on the positive aspects of your life and give negative sentiments less significance. While these wonderful aspects of your life may be floating about in your subconscious, writing them down brings them to life.

More Happiness

When you express thankfulness, you are acknowledging the wonderful things in your life. You may feel more positive emotions, enjoy wonderful experiences, and establish strong relationships by writing these things down– a blueprint for a happier existence. People who write about gratitude are more positive and feel better about their lives in general, according to research.

Less Stress

Grateful people tend to take care of themselves in a way better than someone without gratitude would. This means they live healthier lives in the long run and are thus better able to manage stress. Focusing on feelings of pleasure and satisfaction, according to scientists, naturally reduces stress and leaves you feeling a lot more grounded and capable of dealing with anything life throws at you.

Boosts Self-Esteem

Keeping a journal is a deeply personal hobby that helps you to be fully aware of your own accomplishments. It's been demonstrated that expressing thankfulness reduces social comparisons and that expressing gratitude makes you less inclined to be resentful of others.

Enhanced Sleep Experience

You are far less likely to consider your troubles if you think about the pleasant events of the day or remind yourself of what you have to be thankful for. This clears your thoughts for a good night's sleep.

Increases Resilience

Resilience is an important aspect of our mental health, and thankfulness may play a part here as well. Gratitude can help us overcome trauma as well as reduce stress. If you are going through a huge life transition, thinking about what you're grateful for can help you zoom out of what's going on right now.

Improves Physical Health

We are better equipped to understand the worth of things like physical health when we recognize what we are grateful for. This may drive us to take better care of it, resulting in these incredible results and improved physical health.

These considerations should persuade us to make gratitude a habit in our lives. The simplest approach to keeping track of things is to scribble them down. Some may find it tough to write every day, but it is well worth the effort once the habit is developed.

Each person's thankfulness notebook will be unique. Some people will simply write about their day, while others will concentrate on a particular appreciation quote. The most important thing is that you choose a timetable that suits you and your way of life. There are a few pointers to be taken into consideration when you choose to create gratitude lists.

Choosing a Medium

To start creating a gratitude list, you first need to choose your preference. Ask yourself if you prefer writing it all down on a computer, or go with the good old pen and paper. There are a variety of gratitude journal options available online, as well as traditional journals. Make a choice and make it available to yourself. Traditional journals give the most versatility because they're robust and portable, but notepads can be just as useful for quick workouts or jotting down notes throughout the day. Consider if you'll use it solely for gratitude writing or whether you'll also use it for daily planning. A new diary can sometimes be just what you need to get started.

Spare a Time Slot

Allocate a chunk of your time solely to writing in your gratitude journal. Consider it a fun activity rather than an obligation, and link it to something you currently do. For example, while sipping your morning coffee, you can jot down a list of things for which you are grateful. Alternatively, you may reflect on the events of the day and scribble down the things for which you are grateful just before going to bed.

Think of New Ideas

Because you're writing every day, you could feel like you are running out of things to write on your gratitude list. You can always look for alternative themes and prompts to write about if this happens. It is not just about the things you are grateful for on an everyday basis; it is also about the memories, the moments you have spent with folks, the people you have met, the stuff you own, the accomplishments you have made, your noteworthy qualities and so on. Just remember that it is your journal, and you can write absolutely anything you want, no matter how big or small it is. Do not stop writing just because you are stumped.

Keep a Record of Your Progress

Consider how your happiness has progressed over time. Perhaps your interpersonal interactions have improved, or your self-talk has improved. Return to old pages to discover how far you've come if you ever need a pick- me-up.

Oprah Winfrey, a famous American talk show host, and a philanthropist, advocates the use of a gratitude journal as well. She mentioned in an article on her website that she used to write down the things she was grateful for on a regular basis. However, due to her busy schedule, she stopped with time. She then realized how she did not feel the same pleasure anymore. The root cause of it, according to her, was that she stopped writing things she was grateful for. As a result, Oprah found her way back to this habit no matter how busy she was. She says, "I know for sure that appreciating whatever shows up for you in life changes your personal vibration. You radiate and generate more goodness for yourself when you're aware of all you have and not focusing on your have- nots."

Nothing will be able to stop you once you begin to be grateful for the small things in your life. As a human, you become happier and more optimistic, unaffected by the challenges that life throws at you.

Chapter Ten
Sit In A Positive Company

We have never been taught to filter out our friends and others around us, so we prefer to ignore who we hang out with most of the time. What we don't know is how much of an impact these folks may have on us simply by being in our presence. They may prevent us from reaching our objectives without our knowledge.

Jim Rohn, a famous motivational speaker says, "You are the average of the five people you spend the most time with", and everyone should reflect on this concept and incorporate it into their daily lives. We can have a more optimistic mindset and accomplish more in our work by utilizing the energy of those around us. You will be more inspired and encouraged to keep going if you can harness the optimism of those around you. Because the world can be a harsh place oftentimes, it is critical to surround yourself with positive individuals.

You may ask what a positive person is like and how to know if someone is good company for you. Positive people are cheerful people who use their energy to encourage, inspire, and motivate others. These are people who give true value to us, whether intellectually, emotionally, or spiritually. A family member or friend can be the motivator you need since they can help you succeed by encouraging you and cheering you on. Look for productive employees that aren't easily sidetracked yet are always willing to help you in need.

Another question you might have in your mind is, why is it so essential to surround yourself with these positive people? The answer is quite simple. Positive people's enthusiasm will rub off on you, motivating you to put forth the effort and get ahead of the competitors at work. Following this strategy will help you feel better about your career and be more open to learning, listening, and moving forward. Positive people are more likely to invest in their own future, which can inspire you to work harder to achieve your goals.

It is incredibly essential to remember that likes attract each other, therefore you should radiate positive energy to attract positive people, and vice versa. It is still crucial, however, to be yourself. Set a goal for yourself so you don't feel like you're going around in circles. Setting realistic goals and a challenge for yourself might make you feel more confident that your career is heading in the right direction.

Most of us understand that simply working hard and performing good work isn't enough to get noticed, promoted, or get career progression possibilities that might otherwise go to others. Certainly, we've spoken about how you should focus on your top priorities and take advantage of any available training, but there's also something to be said for maintaining a positive attitude at work. You don't have to adore your job or surround yourself with artificially cheery people, but being happy goes a long way.

Positive people possess a unique blend of habits that can have a positive impact on those around them, and we'll go through a few of them below so we can choose the right people to surround ourselves with.

They Like to Stay Busy

These folks are not inert or idle. They expect things to be completed.

This could be performed on a small or massive scale. This personality feature manifests itself in their personal lives, professional lives, and interpersonal connections.

They Like to Stay Busy

These folks are not inert or idle. They expect things to be completed. This could be performed on a small or massive scale. This personality feature manifests itself in their personal lives, professional lives, and interpersonal connections.

They Make Changes

People that are optimistic do not wait for things to change or be better. They don't blame their lives on their surroundings or other people; instead, they set out to accomplish the changes they desire. They do not even wait for good fortune, miracles, or for things to alter in their favor. They look for solutions to bring about the desired transformation.

They Know When to Let Go

Letting go of the past liberates you from a plethora of oppressive and pointless thoughts and worries, as well as makes you happy.

Positive people have an easier time letting go than negative people because bad thoughts are more difficult to lodge in their minds. They trust their judgment to let go of negative forces in their lives rather than clinging to ideas, beliefs, or even people that are no longer healthy for them.

They Don't Cling to The Past

Both good and unpleasant memories are relegated to the past, where they occurred. Positive people are fully immersed in the current moment and relish it. They are unconcerned about the past or the future. They may make plans for the future, but they recognize that in order to make these goals a reality, they must act now, in the now. If they recall anything from the past, it is to use the lessons learned as stepping stones to a brighter future.

They are Always Grateful

The folks who are the most appreciative are the ones who are the most positive. They could not care less about the snags in their lives. They concentrate on the pot of gold that is waiting for them every day, filled with fresh smells, sights, feelings, and experiences. They look at life as a treasure trove brimming with new opportunities and wonders.

They Do Not Let Their Fears Get in the Way

According to positive people, those who let their worries hold them back never really live an exciting and full life. They move with caution, but they do not allow fear to prevent them from taking risks. They understand that setbacks and complications are an equal part of the process of living a successful life as are achievements and accomplishments. Due to a strong belief in their personal resilience, individuals are certain that they will always get back up when knocked to the ground by life circumstances or their own shortcomings.

They Do Not Play Victim

Believing that you are a victim of incidents reflects a negative attitude regarding yourself and life. It also implies a lack of self-assurance and self- esteem. People that are positive do not allow others to pull their strings. They understand that blaming others for their issues and circumstances will get them nowhere. They trust themselves, are cheerful and confident, and anticipate positive outcomes. This attitude keeps negative thoughts out of their heads and out of their actions.

Positive people also have good communication skills, are always moving forward despite obstacles, are always seeking ways to grow and improve, are not complainers, and create their own opportunities to move forward so that nothing holds them back.

Poverty, illiteracy, and ignorance were all obstacles that Henry Ford had to overcome. Despite his issues, he became one of America's wealthiest men, and much of the credit for this may be attributed to the people he surrounded himself with. For example, he was discovered to be friendly with Thomas Edison.

Harvey Firestone, John Burroughs, and Luther Burbank were among his acquaintances. These individuals were all noted for their brilliant minds. When it came to coordinating with them all, Henry Ford possessed not only a massive amount of brainpower and intelligence, but he also had all of the knowledge, personal experiences, research, and most importantly a positive mindset and motivation that he could possibly employ.

Chapter Eleven

Manifest Your Dreams

Manifestation is the process of attracting something solid into your life by attraction and belief, a process also sometimes referred to as the Law of Attraction. If you believe it, it will happen. However, manifestation is more than just perseverance and optimism. Even while manifesting is all about making your dreams come true, it does necessitate taking proactive efforts toward whatever it is you want. It does not just appear out of nowhere. In fact, it demands a large quantity of time and patience.

However, that is a tiny amount to pay for something that may have such a significant impact on your life. Using the law of attraction to manifest your ambitions is to change your perspective from one of scarcity to one of abundance. The law of attraction is not really a magic wand, after all. We all have layers of confining notions, anxieties, and barriers that are difficult to overcome overnight.

Instead, we must put in the effort to remove the negative patterns that have been stored in our unconscious and replace them with more empowered ones in order to become masters of manifesting via the law of attraction. Just as there is a feasible strategy to do everything, manifestation has its own set of protocols that must be followed in order for it to function properly. We can break it down into a bunch of steps to make it easier to understand.

Know What You Want

You must have a clear idea of what you want. Since you have a better idea of your dreams than anyone else, know what you want and embrace it.

Visualize your Dreams

Consider how your life will change once you achieve your goals. Concentrate on how fulfilling these goals will make you feel. Visualize yourself living your ideal as if it were already true.

Filling in the blanks in step one is critical because it prepares you to face the next two phases in the appropriate mentality. Visualizing an activity activates many of the same brain areas as actually performing it, according to psychologists.

Have Faith in Yourself

How can you expect to make progress if you don't feel you can achieve your goals? Manifesting your desires requires both magic and activity. If you don't believe it's feasible, it won't happen, as we are all taught as children from fairy tales. If you do not have faith in yourself and think something is likely to fail, you will most likely fail.

Students who identified themselves as having poor self-belief, lack of control, and a strong fear of failure had much greater rates of anxiety, cynicism, and lower achievement than their peers who believed in themselves and were not afraid to fail, according to a 2002 study by Andrew Martin.

The action phase of manifesting your dreams isn't always simple, and you'll need that built-in confidence in yourself to get you through the tough times ahead. When things get rough, think about the people you idealize and remember that they did not get where they are by giving up or quitting in the face of adversity; they persevered, and so should you.

Start Working on It

Knowing what you want is only part of the battle action, you won't see any results. Set aside some time to consider what measures you can take to achieve your goals on your own, and then include them in your daily routine. What good is a dream if it isn't accompanied by a strategy?

To lead you where you need to go, the law of attraction works in mysterious ways as well as following logical lines. It's time to establish a plan now that you know exactly what you want and feel you can get it. Look for people who are currently doing what you want to accomplish if you don't know where to begin.

Don't be frightened to accomplish something that has already been done because your contribution will make it more useful and distinctive. Your strategy may evolve over time, but start somewhere and make sure each step advances you forward.

Ask For It

You are now ready to go for your dreams because you know what you want, you believe you can get it, and you have a well-thought-out strategy for achieving it. So, get out there and take action. Because the law of attraction does not function through imagination alone, the natural next step in manifesting your dreams.

It exposes you to new experiences and chances, allowing you to take action and realize your goals. You will also notice that magic happens along the way. You need to ask the universe for what you want once you've determined exactly what your aspirations, dreams, and goals are. This can be done in a variety of ways, including prayer, meditation, visualization, saying your intentions out, and creating a vision board, which is a container filled with photographs of goods you wish to manifest.

Apart from the steps, you may need to make minor adjustments to your daily routine and general behavior to achieve the results you desire. Small habits incorporated into your usual life might make the manifestation process go much more smoothly and effectively. Some of these habits are listed below.

Be Grateful

Even if you do not get everything you want in the order or time period you want, you should accept and appreciate what you do get—no matter how big or tiny it is. Consider keeping a gratitude journal to help you with this. Spend five to ten minutes before bedtime writing down a few things you are thankful for, as well as anything that happened that day to help you get closer to whatever it is you're attempting to manifest.

Eliminate the Negative Energy

You must remove any hurdles or limiting ideas that may cloud your vision, such as fear and negative self-talk, in addition to changing your thinking and behaviors. Before you can move past your limiting beliefs, you must first figure out what they are.

Identify your beliefs and thoughts by questioning yourself. It's simpler to remember them if you write them down. Then cross off any that you believe are obstructing your view or holding you back. Replacing these limiting beliefs with newer, more positive affirmations is a good idea. For example, if you believe "I am not good enough," replace it with "I am amazing and enough"

Keep a Track of Your Energy

You receive the energy that you expend. You will attract the same bad emotion if you put negative energy out through your thoughts and feelings. The law of attraction works in this way. On the other hand, if you can alter your energy, you'll attract more positivity, which will assist you in achieving your goals.

Fortunately, altering your energy is a basic and straightforward process. All you have to do is include activities that make you happy and give you great energy. This varies from person to person since different things bring happiness to different people. If assisting others makes you happy, for example, aim to help at least one person every day.

You can also reward yourself with some well-deserved self-care by practicing meditation or doing anything else that soothes you every day.

Make Sure You Know Your Dreams

We do not always know what our dreams are. Perhaps we want to make a lot of money but we do not know how to. The good part, although, is the fact that there are ways you can use to tap into your subconscious mind and generate ideas for manifesting your desires. As a result, the outcomes are frequently surprising, and they will assist you in discovering skills and ideas that you would not have considered if you had simply sat down and forced yourself to think about them. These include:

- Meditation: Meditation is a wonderful method for clearing your mind of distracting thoughts and finding clarity.
- Vision Board: Vision boards are a wonderful, creative way to figure out what you want out of life. They're an excellent starting step toward making your dreams a reality. All you have to do is make a collage of words and images from different sources on a board that expresses your personality and flair. These are things you would like to have in your life. Put this board up somewhere you'll see it every day.
- Journaling: Another technique to help clarify your dreams is to write them down on paper. It's possible that once you start writing, your dreams will diverge from what you thought you wanted.

Have the Impression that You Already Have All You Desire

The feeling is the same as believing. Allow yourself to be transported to a world where everything has gone your way. Pay attention to the small things: how this world looks, feels, and sounds. This will make you feel more energized and positive and will motivate you to keep taking inspired action toward your goals.

The feeling is the same as believing. Allow yourself to be transported to a world where everything has gone your way. Pay attention to the small things: how this world looks, feels, and sounds. This will make you feel more energized and positive and will motivate you to keep taking inspired action toward your goals.

Have the Impression that You Already Have All You Desire

The feeling is the same as believing. Allow yourself to be transported to a world where everything has gone your way. Pay attention to the small things: how this world looks, feels, and sounds. This will make you feel more energized and positive and will motivate you to keep taking inspired action toward your goals.

The feeling is the same as believing. Allow yourself to be transported to a world where everything has gone your way. Pay attention to the small things: how this world looks, feels, and sounds. This will make you feel more energized and positive and will motivate you to keep taking inspired action toward your goals.

The famous Oprah Winfrey, who grew up in the face of adversity, is an example of how well manifesting may work. Despite the challenges, she believed she was capable of great things. If you tell yourself a story often enough, it will become true. That is precisely what occurred. The exquisite woman went on to become the first Black female billionaire in the world.

She created opportunities for herself long before she had a name. Oprah sets the bar for manifesting because she has become so wise as a result of her achievements, but her results are replicable. She also encourages people to follow her lead and live the life they desire. She was known to employ vision boards as well.

Chapter Twelve
Indulge in Mental & Physical Exercise

Physical and mental health are two facets of one's overall well-being. These are things you can improve on at any time for the sake of your health. However, due to their hectic schedules, many nowadays tend to overlook these factors, not recognizing that poor health can affect their work effectiveness and prevent them from performing at their best. It is about time we start focusing on our physical and mental health and this can be done by indulging in physical as well as mental exercises. It may take some time but is well worth the effort.

Physical Exercise

Although everyone is aware that physical activity is good for our health, many of us are unaware of the numerous benefits that occur as a result of it. Following are a few prominent benefits of physical health.

Combats Health Conditions

Being active increases high-density lipoprotein (HDL) cholesterol, which is the healthy kind of cholesterol, and lowers harmful triglycerides, regardless of your current weight. This two-pronged approach maintains your blood flowing freely, lowering your risk of cardiovascular disease.

Regular exercise can help you avoid or manage a variety of health issues. Examples are stroke, high blood pressure, type 2 diabetes, arthritis, high cholesterol, as well depression, and anxiety.

Better Mood

Physical activity triggers the release of chemicals in the brain that make you feel happier, more relaxed, and less nervous. It causes alterations in the brain areas that control stress and anxiety. It can also improve brain sensitivity to the neurotransmitters serotonin and norepinephrine, which help to alleviate depressive symptoms. Moreover, exercising can also boost the production of endorphins, which are known to assist promote happy feelings and lower pain perception.

Boosts Energy

Regular physical activity can help you strengthen your muscles and increase your stamina. Exercise helps your cardiovascular system perform more efficiently by delivering oxygen and nutrients to your tissues. You'll have more energy to tackle daily duties as your heart and lung health improves.

Controls Weight

Regular exercise has been demonstrated to raise your metabolic rate, which can help you lose weight by burning more calories. The higher the intensity of your activity, the more calories you will burn.

Better Skin Health

Frequent light exercise can boost your body's natural antioxidant production, which helps protect cells. Similarly, exercise can increase blood flow and cause skin cell adaptations, which can assist to delay the onset of skin aging.

Helps Brain Health and Memory

Exercise can help protect memory and thinking skills while also improving brain function. To start with, it raises your heart rate, allowing more blood and oxygen to reach your brain. It can also increase the synthesis of hormones that promote brain cell proliferation.

Furthermore, because the chronic disease can influence your brain's function, exercise's ability to avoid chronic disease can translate into benefits for your brain. Exercise has been proven to increase the size of the hippocampus, a brain region important for memory and learning, which may assist enhance mental performance in older persons.

Good for Bones and Muscles

Exercise is essential for the development and maintenance of strong muscles and bones. When combined with proper protein intake, activities like weightlifting can help you gain muscle. This is because exercise promotes the production of hormones that aid in the absorption of amino acids by your muscles.

This promotes their growth and minimizes the likelihood of them breaking down. People lose muscle mass and strength as they age, which can contribute to an increased risk of injury. Regular physical activity is critical for preventing muscle loss and preserving strength as you become older.

Exercise also aids in the development of bone density in children and the prevention of osteoporosis later in life.

Relaxation and Better Sleep

Because exercise depletes a large percentage of your energy, it stimulates restorative processes during sleep, which enhances sleep quality. Furthermore, it is hypothesized that the increase in body temperature that occurs during exercise improves sleep quality by allowing the body temperature to decline during sleep.

After evaluating all of the benefits of physical activity, we should be persuaded to continue with it and incorporate it into our everyday lives, giving it the same priority as eating and working. We can always experiment with different workouts to see what works best for us.

There are a variety of exercises that may be done at various levels of difficulty based on the benefit we want to get or the sections of our body we want to target. Most people concentrate on one sort of exercise or activity and believe that this is sufficient. It's crucial to obtain all four forms of exercise, according to research: endurance, strength, balance, and flexibility.

Each one has its own set of advantages. Doing one type can help you enhance your ability to do the others, and variety can help you avoid boredom and injury. You can choose activities that suit your fitness level and needs regardless of your age!

- Endurance Exercises: Endurance exercises increase your breathing and heart rates. These exercises help you stay healthy, develop your fitness, and do the duties you need to do on a daily basis. These include brisk walking, jogging, swimming, dancing, and even climbing stairs, among others.

Strength Exercises: Muscle strength can make a significant difference. Keeping your muscles strong might help you maintain your balance and avoid falls and injuries. Weight lifting is referred to as "strength training" or "resistance training" by certain people. Some examples

> would be, lifting weights or grocery bags, wall pushups, arm curls, and using resistance bands.

- Balance Exercises: Balance exercises assist older persons to avoid falls, which are a prevalent problem with devastating implications. These include the balance walk, trying to balance on one foot, etc.
- Stretching Exercises: Stretching can help you become more flexible. These can be the back stretch exercise, and the ankle stretches, among others.

Mental Exercise

Our emotional, psychological, and social well-being are all part of our mental health. It has an impact on the way we think, feels, and behave. It also influences how we deal with stress, interacts with others, and make decisions. Mental health is vital at all stages of life, including childhood, adolescence, and maturity. As a result, it is critical that we prioritize our mental health at all times and ensure that we are mentally active and healthy. Given how crucial your mental health is in every element of your life, it's critical to protect and develop your mental health through suitable measures, and one of them is a mental exercise.

We have already talked about how physical activity can improve your mental health by making you happy and helping you combat depression and anxiety; we will now discuss how mental exercises can significantly improve our mental wellness by making our brains stronger.

Brain training is advertised as a means to sharpen your intellect and possibly increase intelligence. While many cognitive scientists believe that the claims made about brain training are overblown and misleading, there is a growing body of evidence showing some activities can be favorable to your brain's functioning. Here are a few ways to do that.

Stay Physically Healthy

You must first take care of your body before you can take care of your mind. Start with improving your physical health if you want to improve your mental health. Go for a stroll, start eating more fresh fruits and vegetables, and attempt to break any unhealthy habits you may have, such as excessive alcohol or tobacco usage. Some of these will be tougher than others, but your brain will reward you for it for years.

Learn New Things

Learning something new is one method to keep your brain active and offer new challenges on a regular basis. Learning a new language, learning to play a musical instrument, or picking up a new pastime are all possibilities. You will not only be stretching your mind, but you will also be learning something new as you continue to grow your talents and achieve more success.

Meditation

Meditation is a brain activity you may not have considered, but it can be highly beneficial. Mindfulness meditation, in particular, is all the vogue right now, with cognitive psychologists, business executives, and various healthcare practitioners touting its benefits. Meditation has been found to increase the thickness of the prefrontal cortex. Higher-order brain functions, such as greater awareness, focus, and decision-making, are managed by this brain area. Higher-order brain functions become stronger as a result of meditation, whereas lower-order brain processes decline.

Tai Chi

It is no secret that tai chi has numerous health benefits, including mental health. It can also help you find your core when your life is out of whack. Practicing tai chi on a daily basis can help you relax, sleep better, and improve your memory. Long-term tai chi practice can cause structural changes in the brain, resulting in an increase in brain volume, according to a 2013 study.

There are many other ways of mental exercise such as playing brain games and puzzles. Certain brain exercises that improve memory, concentration, and focus can help you complete daily chores faster and more easily, as well as maintain your mind fresh as you age.

Chapter Thirteen
Rebuilding Your Motivation

Life is about unexpected turns that can lead you to a different road. That is when we feel there is no sense of credibility, and it wasn't an exam we prepared for. The questions are all out of the syllabus, and losing motivation feels like the only option.

We need to remember that we are in control of our lives, and it is up to us what we make of it. We can choose to be discouraged by the situation and let it take over, or rise to the challenge and do something great. The decision is always ours, and it starts with believing in ourselves.

This is how we remember to rebuild our motivation- always heading up to the top, unprepared and challenged. We need to start with the end goal in mind and think about everything we can do to get there. Sometimes it's helpful to break down the goal into smaller steps and take the time to celebrate each accomplishment along the way.

We have to be patient with ourselves because it takes time and dedication to reach our goals. No one can expect to do everything perfectly the first time around, but we can learn and grow from our mistakes.

When we focus on what we want to achieve, it gives us the strength to keep going even when things get tough. We can find comfort in knowing that we are doing something worthwhile and that the journey is worth taking. The most important thing is to never lose sight of our dreams. They are what inspire us to be better people and to do great things.

"When you get into a tight place and everything goes against you, till it seems as though you could not hang on a minute longer, never give up then, for that is just the place and time that the tide will turn." –Harriet Beecher Stowe

What Can Make You Feel Demotivated And A Limited Person?

There are a few things that can make you feel demotivated and limited.

One of those things is not having a clear plan or goal in your life.

When you don't have anything to strive for, it's easy to feel like you're not capable of achieving great things.

Another thing that can make you feel this way is feeling like you're not good enough. If you don't believe in yourself, it's going to be tough to accomplish anything great.

Lastly, comparison can be a major factor in feeling demotivated. When you're constantly comparing yourself to others, it's easy to feel like you're not good enough.

Remember that everyone is unique and special in their own way. Focus on your own journey and don't worry about what everyone else is doing.

Rebuild Your Motivation As A No-Limit Person

So you've been plugging away at your goals for a while now, but all of the sudden you find yourself struggling to keep your motivation afloat. It's not unusual to experience a lull in motivation every once in a while, but if it becomes a regular occurrence then it can be tough to make any real progress. Fortunately, there are a few things you can do to rebuild your motivation when it starts to dwindle.

Set Some Smaller Goals To Shoot For

To rebuild your motivation, set smaller goals that you can accomplish more easily. This will help you to feel more successful and motivated, and it can also help to keep you on track with your larger goals. Setting smaller goals allows you to break down the larger goal into more manageable chunks, which makes it easier to stay focused and motivated. Plus, when you achieve your smaller goals, you'll be one step closer to reaching your ultimate goal.

The best way to not feel hopeless is to get up and do something. Don't wait for good things to happen to you. If you go out and make some good things happen, you will fill the world with hope, you will fill yourself with hope." – Barack Obama

Take Some Time For Yourself.

When you're feeling overwhelmed or stressed out, it can be hard to stay motivated. In these cases, it's often helpful to take some time for yourself so that you can relax and recharge. This can help you to come back to your goals, feeling more motivated and inspired.

When you find yourself stuck in a corner, with too many struggles around you, it is time to hold your head up high. The more you surround yourself with a toxic environment, the more you will be pulled down. So, take a break and come back stronger than ever.

Find A Support Group.

If you're struggling to stay motivated, find a support group of people who are also working towards similar goals. This can provide you with some much- needed motivation and inspiration. It can also help to keep you accountable.

Support groups include like-minded people who are willing to help each other out and offer feedback. It is a great way to get connected with people who can help you achieve your goals and rebuild your motivation.

Set Some Deadlines.

If you find that you're struggling to stay motivated, set some deadlines for yourself. Giving yourself a timeline for a project can help you stay on track and make sure that you don't procrastinate. This can provide you with a sense of urgency and motivation, and it can also help you to stay on track with your goals.

When you have a set deadline, it is easier to stay focused and motivated. You will know exactly what you need to do in order to reach your goal by the set date. Plus, you'll be less likely to procrastinate when you have a timeline to follow.

Make A Plan.

Make a plan for how you will get back on track. This can help to give you some structure and direction. When you have a plan, it is easier to stay focused and motivated. You might find yourself distracted, demotivated and without a pathway to follow which leads to making more mistakes.

Making a plan can help to simplify things and make them less overwhelming. It will also give you a roadmap to follow so that you can achieve your goals. Plus, having a plan in place makes it easier to track your progress and make adjustments as needed.

Reward Yourself For Your Accomplishments.

When you accomplish something small, reward yourself every time. This can help to keep you motivated and inspired, and it can also make your accomplishments feel more rewarding. Make sure to choose rewards that are meaningful and satisfying to you. When you have something to look forward to after completing a task, you're more likely to stay on track and be successful.

Take Some Time To Reflect On Your Progress.

By taking some time to reflect on your progress so far, you realize certain aspects of life that are conquerable which you thought weren't. This can help you to see how far you've come. You continue working towards your goals. You become a person who takes interest in the slightest changes in your life, making you more focused.

When you take some time to reflect on your progress, It can help to boost your motivation and inspire you to continue working hard. Plus, reflection can help you identify what strategies have been most effective for you and what areas you need to improve on.

Visualize Yourself Achieving Your Goals.

When you're struggling to stay motivated, visualization can be a powerful tool. By visualizing yourself achieving your goals, you can tap into your inner motivation and inspiration. This can help to keep you focused and motivated along the way.

Visualization is a technique that involves picturing yourself achieving your goals in your mind. When you do this, you can feel the excitement, happiness, and satisfaction that come with achieving your goals. This can help to keep you motivated and inspired to continue working hard.

Set Some New Goals.

When you are ready to take the steering wheel of your life in your hands, it is time to set some new goals. These goals should be something that inspires you, and they should also be challenging yet achievable.

When you have new goals to work towards, you'll have more motivation to stay on track. You can give less time to negative thoughts that come with procrastination and more time to rebuild your motivation.

De-Stress With A Hobby

Last but not least, rebuild your motivation by indulging in your favorite hobby. This can help to clear your mind and restore your energy levels.

When you have a hobby that you love, it is easy to get lost. This can help to take your mind off of your goals and the tasks you need to complete to achieve them. You can de-stress and recharge your batteries while boosting your motivation.

Chapter Fourteen
Acknowledge Your Internal Feelings

> *"We can never obtain peace in the outer world until we make peace with ourselves"*
> *(Dalai Lama)*

Acknowledging something means recognizing and believing its existence. When it comes to feelings, some of us act dumb while some are God-gifted. They know their way around words like nobody else. But first comes first, you can never be good at acknowledging other people's feelings when you can't even acknowledge your internal feelings. Whatever peace we may desire from the outside world, has to be founded in ourselves first.

There are a million factors, stats, and figures that clearly state that there is a risk in this possible scenario, yet we can't kick that idea from our minds, because that's how we are made. We were made to ask questions, innovate and adapt. In earlier times, no one was bounded by anything. There was no racism and everybody stood on the same ground.

Factors that hold and drag us down in society make us bound by a set of rules. These rules are not meant to demotivate anyone in general. These were made while keeping in mind the negative company and the worst possible scenarios. A kid growing up in such a way, won't ever trust anyone from outside and he will create a sense of superiority over them. This is not the way that humans should be treated and raised.

"Birds born in a cage think flying is an illness" (Alejandro Jodorowsky)

When you acknowledge your internal feelings, true betterment and improvement follow. You can't deny the existence of something that is actually present. Acknowledging your internal feelings means accepting the possible presence of feelings for something and someone. One simply can't improve, if he/she feels that they don't require improvement. Firstly, you need to analyze and look at yourself. You need to ask yourself that after a decade if I look back at this current state, will I be pleased and satisfied with myself, or I will scratch my head.

Acknowledging your internal feelings for someone and something makes you goal-oriented. We have the example of a legendary player of soccer; Cristiano Ronaldo. He was born in a poor family and his father was an alcoholic. He never really understood, why his dad drank so much. He was not good at studies, but he was exceptional in sports. At the age of 13-19, a lot of teenagers think about careers and how they can't focus on a specific goal. Goal orientation is a skill that is missing in a lot of teenagers nowadays.

Icon of football, Cristiano Ronaldo acknowledged his internal feelings for the love of soccer. He trained by himself and chose the career of a professional footballer. Less than 5% of the people are selected as Pro Athletes and CR7 believed in himself. He wanted to prove his haters wrong and make life easier for his family. He wanted to chase his passion. He could have failed miserably as we risked it all. But he was selected as a Pro athlete and is now the G.O.A.T of football.

There are so many examples of people who didn't let fear reach into their skulls, and their continuous hustle made them who they are today. It is always easy to give up, you have the back of your loved ones and thus you have an option to just give up any hustle for an opportunity. But when you don't have anybody to rely upon, you just risk your life on the chance, you believe in GO FAST or GO HOME. You consider it your last attempt at redemption and you give it your all.

Many people suffer from borderline personality disorder (BPD), and some other psychiatric disorders. These involve intense emotional experiences and having trouble accepting emotions. Without a shadow of a doubt, it is very hard to deal with emotions that are painful and scary. However, accepting your emotions can actually help you a lot. It can improve your emotion regulation and lead to fewer mood swings that result in more emotional balance.

When we are uncomfortable and feel emotions, such as sadness, fear, or shame, we just want to get rid of that feeling asap. These feelings drag a lot of people down a road where there is no way to return. To avoid such feelings, people use drugs and alcohol and they think that it might help them in avoiding the thoughts, but as drugs are slow poison, they start killing the person from the inside. When you are not worried about dying from drugs, you develop this attitude that doesn't let you get affected by anything said or done.

No one wants to walk around feeling pain all the time. Although a little reminders keep us on track, suffering the whole time is no one's desire. When we give a reaction towards something, it is sometimes positive and sometimes negative. So, rejecting the way we feel about something, makes things worse for us, emotions of all types arise inside us and it doesn't let us keep a straight mind. Emotions that proved helpful, don't ever help you, sometimes they become your worst nightmare. You can't just bury a dream or feeling that is in your heart.

Everything works perfectly when it is in order. Same is the case for internal feelings and emotions. You need to keep them under control at all times. To keep everything in order, first, you need to know about it. So, if you want to keep your internal feelings in control and acknowledge them, you would have to know them first. To acknowledge your inner feelings, you need to step ahead of any obstacles and you need to place no boundary on yourself. Let yourself be completely free. After doing that, the thoughts that just keep popping in your head are the real deal. If you are thinking about career or field to choose, just think that you have to work in that specific field for the rest of your life and the field that pops up at that time is your real deal.

There are moments in our life that demand total honesty with others and even our own self, at those times, you just have to tell your inner feelings. If you haven't even acknowledged your internal feelings, you are left in a state of dilemma. You can't choose anything. You don't feel true to yourself. Without acknowledging your internal feelings, how can anyone be sure about anything. To get out of this unending labyrinth, we have to know and acknowledge our internal feelings.

Acknowledging internal feelings means to accept feelings and being ready for whatever comes out. It is not always in your favor and this is this biggest reason why most people are afraid of going all out. They are just afraid that they might encounter something vicious. It is simply impossible to get rid of emotions and talking about emotions, we will make terrible decisions without emotions. Imagine not having humanity or sympathy in your mind while making decisions.

Summarizing the whole vibe of acknowledging the internal feeling and emotions. When you acknowledge your internal feelings, true betterment and improvement follow us on the path. We can't deny the existence of something that is actually present in reality. Acknowledging your internal feelings means accepting the presence of feelings for something and reaction towards something or someone. We can't live a life of our choice without acknowledging our internal feelings and emotions. We need to decide whether we will follow for the rest of our life or are we going to lead the whole pack. Being an alpha is not easy, but it is worth it.

Some horrible health issues are dealt with the free flow of internal feelings. These include extreme emotional experiences and having trouble while accepting emotions. Without a shadow of a doubt, it is extremely hard to deal with emotions that are horribly painful and scary. However, if we accept our emotions, they can actually help us a lot. To unlock your inner feelings, you need to step up in front of any obstacles and you need to place no boundary on yourself. Let yourself be completely free. You need to be clutch in situations that demand clutch performance.

If you haven't even acknowledged your internal feelings, then what is the purpose of your life. You can't choose anything specifically. You don't feel true or good about yourself. Without unlocking your internal feelings and emotions, how can anyone be sure when taking decisions. According to some people, meditation and spending time with yourself is the best solution for unlocking true potential and a clear passage way for internal feelings to flow.

Without the free flow of thoughts and boundaries in everything, bound us while making decisions. It is simply impossible to get rid of emotions. If we cut off humanity while taking decisions, it would be morally wrong. Ideal situations and clutch performances require free flow of thoughts and these can only be unlocked if we acknowledge our internal feelings.

Chapter Fifteen
Give Yourself a Due Rest

Allowing yourself to relax is often the most constructive thing you can do. Tragically, this is not always as simple or natural as it appears. We disregard our bodies' warnings to slow down as adults, and then complain about how our productivity has been going down. Nowadays, people consider being busy something to be proud of. This is because we have always been led to believe that keeping yourself busy with things may represent your self-worth in one way or another since the busier you are, the more things you can get done. However, this is not true at all. How much you can accomplish does not make you worthy. There are a number of things you may do to reduce your workload and allow yourself time for relaxation and regeneration. Following are some ways you can incorporate into your busy lives to make things more manageable for yourself and give yourself the rest that you deserve.

Get Your Priorities Straight

Our busyness is frequently the result of trying to manage every part of life as if it were the most essential. However, the reality is that not everything is a major priority. Even if it bothers someone, you must take the time to prioritize what is most important to you. Prioritizing the vital things and understanding what comes first will help you arrange your time more effectively. Instead of juggling everything as if it were all of the same importance, you will be able to devote more time to the most important tasks and less to the ones that can wait. Knowing where to concentrate your efforts quickly reduces your feeling of being overworked. Prioritizing necessitates making something more essential than anything else for a set length of time. Certain activities are valued more highly than others by everyone. This ensures that you do not devote all of your time to getting everything done and that you do not deprive yourself of the rest that you would otherwise receive if you aligned your daily chores from most important to least important.

Learn to Say No

We have been conditioned to say yes to everything our entire lives. So, if your boss keeps increasing your workload and assigning you more and more responsibilities, you keep saying yes because we have been taught that we should do everything happily and without hesitation, and not being able to or not wanting to do everything we are told somehow makes us incompetent. It's time to master the art of saying no, and it is also a lot easier than you might assume. Do not let guilt or the fear of missing out compel you to say yes. If you do not learn to say no, you will always find yourself stacked with more chores than you are willing to do. This means you will be overburdened with tasks to which you could have easily said no to, and you will become exhausted. It will take a huge chunk of your time that you could otherwise spend on getting a good, well-deserved rest.

Connect With Nature:

According to recent studies, being in nature helps our body stay healthy and relieve depression, anxiety, and ADHD. In addition to that, exposure to nature promotes contentment and also lets you feel better emotionally.

There are numerous approaches to interacting with nature, such as taking a walk, sitting on a bench while you read a book, or you can find a quiet space to connect with nature.

In addition to that, you can consider Meditation to calm your thoughts and emotions. Meditating outside has a positive impact that you can feel connections to the environment. While connecting with nature, ensure to turn off your smartphone as it can be a source of interruption.

Conclusion

As we grow older, we constantly hear others preach about how essential it is to live a good life and make the most of it. Some people, on the other hand, are unfamiliar with the concept of a good life and how it works. They believe that those who have a nice life have it easy.

This is not the case, unfortunately. In order to live a good life, you must adopt specific behaviors and alter your mindset. It takes a long time, but it is well worth the effort. This eBook is all about the barriers that keep us from achieving our goals and how to overcome them.

Possess an amazing level of control over all aspects of your life. Enjoy each day to the utmost, free of preoccupations with the past or the future. Separate yourself from outside criticism. To deal efficiently with ordinary disappointments and problems, pay attention to internal cues.

We have now reached the end of the eBook. The eBook covered life's limitations and how to overcome them in order to become the ideal non-limit person who is unafraid of anything and only advances forward. I hope this eBook has assisted you in identifying the factors that may be preventing you from achieving your goals, and that it has also encouraged you to overcome these obstacles.

I hope you found it interesting. From our end, we bid you farewell. Make sure to tell your friends, family, and coworkers about it if they need help getting their lives in order and recognizing the destructive patterns that are getting in the way.

"I would now like to have your sincere opinion expressed on Amazon. Not to feed my ego but rather to tell me what this book has brought you, what you might have liked less, what you may have missed, so that I can further enrich this work which will evolve over time since I will continue to update it

Copyright © 2022 - A Book for a Day

All rights reserved. No part of this publication may be reproduced, distributed, or transmitted in any form or by any means, including photocopying, recording, or other electronic or mechanical methods, without the prior written permission of the publisher, except in the case of brief quotations embodied in critical reviews and certain other noncommercial uses permitted by copyright law. Any references to historical events, real people, or real places can be real or used fictitiously to respect anonymity. Names, characters, and places can be products of the author's imagination.

Printed by Amazon.

Printed in Great Britain
by Amazon